spot

BABY ANIMALS

BABY WOLVES

by K.C. Kelley

AMICUS

eyes

fur

Look for these words and pictures as you read.

nose

pack

Peekaboo!
It's a baby wolf!

A baby wolf is called a pup.
They drink their mother's milk.
Soon they will eat meat!

nose

Look at the pup's nose.
Wolves can smell well.
Their nose helps them find food.

fur

Look at the pup's fur.
Wolves live in cold places.
Fur keeps them warm.

See its eyes?
Baby wolves have blue eyes.
Their eyes will become brown.

eyes

pack

See the pack?

Wolves live in packs.

Most packs have six to 10 wolves.

Adults care for the cubs.

Wolf pups are born in spring.
Soon, they will leave the den.
Time to play!

See its eyes?
Baby wolves have blue eyes.
Their eyes will become brown.

eyes

Look at the pup's fur.
Wolves live in cold places.
Fur keeps them warm.

fur

eyes

fur

Did you find?

nose

pack

Look at the pup's nose.
Wolves can smell well.
Their nose helps them find food.

nose

See the pack.
Wolves live in packs.
Most packs have six to 10 wolves.
Adults care for the cubs.

pack

spot

Amicus Readers and Amicus Ink are imprints of Amicus
P.O. Box 1329, Mankato, MN 56002
www.amicuspublishing.us

Library of Congress Cataloging-in-Publication Data

Names: Kelley, K. C., author.
Title: Baby wolves / by K.C. Kelley.
Description: Mankato, MN : Amicus, [2018] | Series: Spot.
    Baby animals | Description based on print version record and
    CIP data provided by publisher; resource not viewed.
Identifiers: LCCN 2017022575 (print) | LCCN 2017034357
    (ebook) | ISBN 9781681522517 (pdf) | ISBN 9781681513171
    (library binding : alk. paper) | ISBN 9781681522517 (pbk. :
    alk. paper)
Subjects: LCSH: Wolves--Infancy--Juvenile literature.
Classification: LCC QL737.C22 (ebook) | LCC QL737.C22 K45
    2018 (print) | DDC 599.773/139--dc23
LC record available at https://lccn.loc.gov/2017022575

Printed in China

HC   10 9 8 7 6 5 4 3 2 1
PB   10 9 8 7 6 5 4 3 2 1

Megan Peterson, editor
Deb Miner, series designer
Patty Kelley, book designer
Producer/Photo Research:
Shoreline Publishing Group LLC

Photos:
Cover: Isselee/Dreamstime.com.
Inside: Isselee 1, 8; Lynn Bostrom
2tl, 3, 6; Mikael Males 2tr; Holly
Kuchara 2bl; Mrrphotography
2bl; Jens Klingbiel 10. Minden
Pictures: Justin and Christine Sohns
12. Shutterstock: Holly Kuchara 4,
Bildagentur Zoonar GmbH 14.

BABY WOLVES